FORMING OUR NATION

Establishing the Judicial Branch

by Tyler Omoth

LIGHTBOX
openlightbox.com

LIGHTBOX

Go to **www.openlightbox.com** and enter this book's unique code.

ACCESS CODE

LBXZ9437

Lightbox is an all-inclusive digital solution for the teaching and learning of curriculum topics in an original, groundbreaking way. Lightbox is based on National Curriculum Standards.

STANDARD FEATURES OF LIGHTBOX

AUDIO High-quality narration using text-to-speech system

ACTIVITIES Printable PDFs that can be emailed and graded

SLIDESHOWS Pictorial overviews of key concepts

VIDEOS Embedded high-definition video clips

WEBLINKS Curated links to external, child-safe resources

TRANSPARENCIES Step-by-step layering of maps, diagrams, charts, and timelines

INTERACTIVE MAPS Interactive maps and aerial satellite imagery

QUIZZES Ten multiple choice questions that are automatically graded and emailed for teacher assessment

KEY WORDS Matching key concepts to their definitions

Establishing the Judicial Branch

Contents

CHAPTER 1

A New Government

The American Revolutionary War (1775–1783) was finally over. The United States was now **independent**. But in 1783, the U.S. government did not look the way it does today. It was made up of one main body. This body was known as the Congress of the Confederation.

After the last British soldier evacuated New York City, General George Washington marched into the city on November 25, 1783.

Many important meetings took place at the Pennsylvania State House, now known as Independence Hall, in Philadelphia.

The government had little power over the states. For instance, the Congress could not make the states follow the laws it created. And there was nobody to solve disagreements about existing laws.

In 1787, U.S. leaders called for a meeting in Philadelphia, Pennsylvania. They hoped this meeting would fix the **federal** government. But some people at the meeting wanted to create a whole new government. To do so, they would write a new constitution.

One plan became popular. Created by James Madison, it was known as the Virginia Plan. It said the new government would not have just one body. Instead, the government would split power between three branches. The legislative branch, known as Congress, would create laws. The executive branch would make sure people obeyed these laws. And the judicial branch would settle disagreements about the laws.

James Madison's Virginia Plan was the framework for what became the U.S. Constitution.

Members of the meeting to create the Constitution debated for four months. Compromise was finally reached on September 17, 1787.

The judicial branch would be the nation's highest court. But the people at the meeting argued about several points. For example, would there be one court or many? Would the court review every law? Some people worried that the federal courts would be too powerful if they could undo acts of the legislative branch.

In the end, the people at the meeting decided on one high court. They also agreed to the possibility of lower federal courts. In addition, the judicial branch would not review every law. But it would have the power to compare laws to the Constitution. If a law did not follow the Constitution, the law would be struck down.

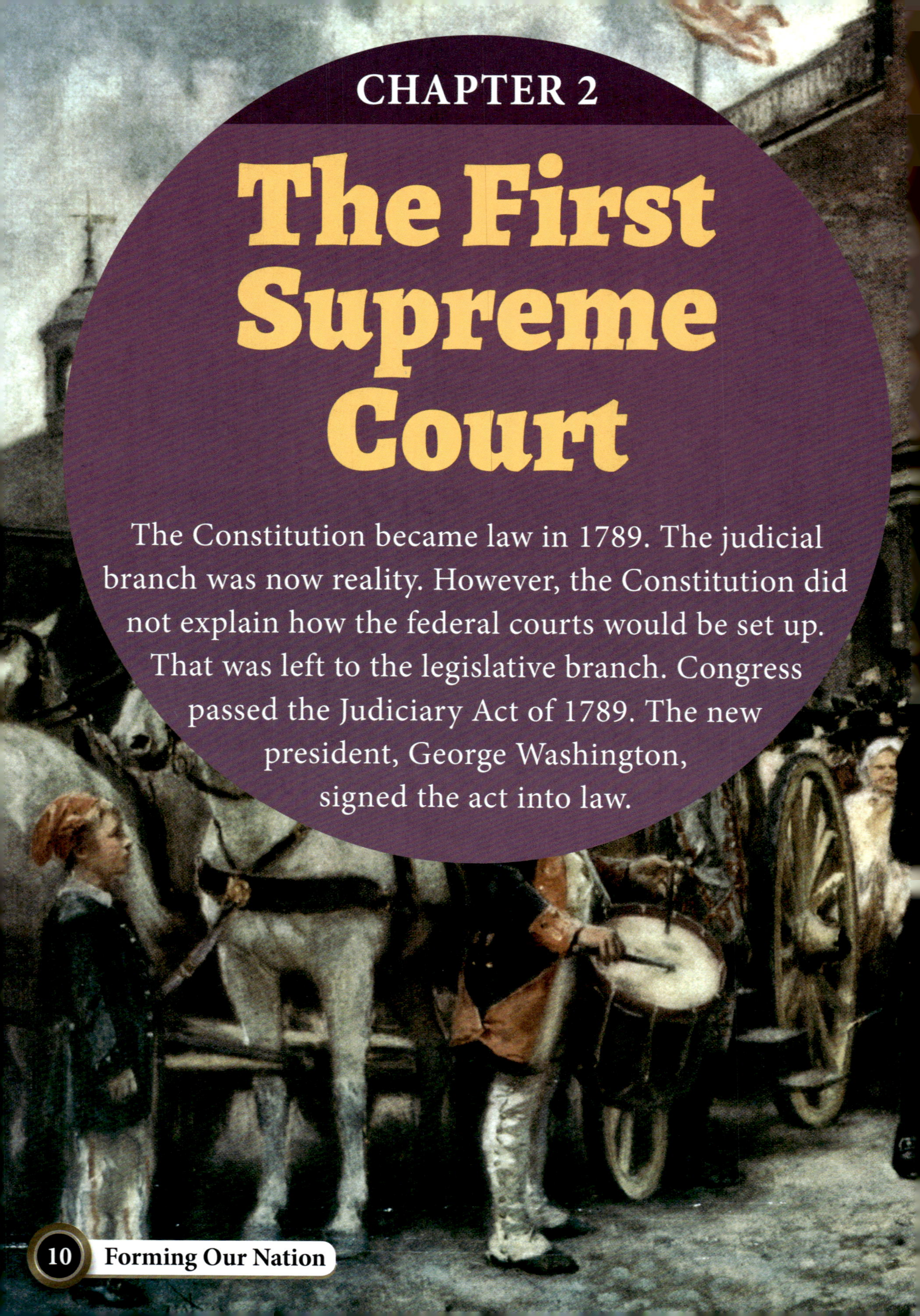

CHAPTER 2

The First Supreme Court

The Constitution became law in 1789. The judicial branch was now reality. However, the Constitution did not explain how the federal courts would be set up. That was left to the legislative branch. Congress passed the Judiciary Act of 1789. The new president, George Washington, signed the act into law.

In 1789, George Washington became the first U.S. president and leader of the executive branch.

The act created three levels to the federal court system. The top level was the Supreme Court. This court started out with six **justices**. Below this level, there were three circuit courts. Each circuit court was ruled by three justices. Two were from the Supreme Court, and one was from the district courts. The district courts were the lowest level. They were spread out among the states.

The Supreme Court justices were **appointed** by the president. Then the Senate had to approve them. Each justice would serve for the rest of his or her life.

Early Federal Courts

The Judiciary Act of 1789 outlined the country's judicial system. It started with 13 district courts, one for each state.

They were overseen by three circuit courts, which served the northern states, middle states, and southern states. Above them all was the Supreme Court.

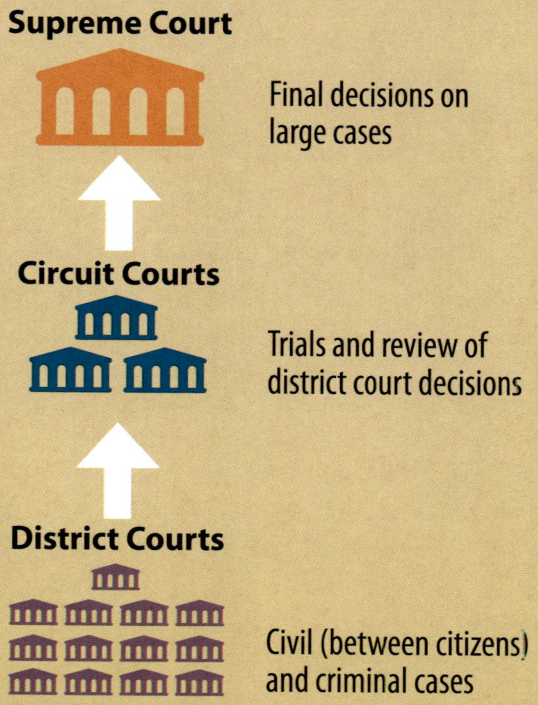

As the first president, Washington had to fill all the positions in the federal court. He thought carefully about his appointments. He believed the Supreme Court was important to the country.

Others saw the judicial branch as the weakest part of the new government. Many justices were not excited about joining the court.

Federal Judge FACTS

While president, *George Washington* appointed **38** federal judges.

The first federal judges started work **two days** after the *Judiciary Act* was passed in **1789**.

The first *district court judges* made up to **$1,800** a year. *Chief justices* made up to **$4,000**.

CHAPTER 3

Judging the Early Years

In 1790, the Supreme Court gathered for the first time. The justices met in New York City. John Jay of New York led the court. He was the first chief justice. However, the court was not busy in its early days. It did not have any cases until its second year.

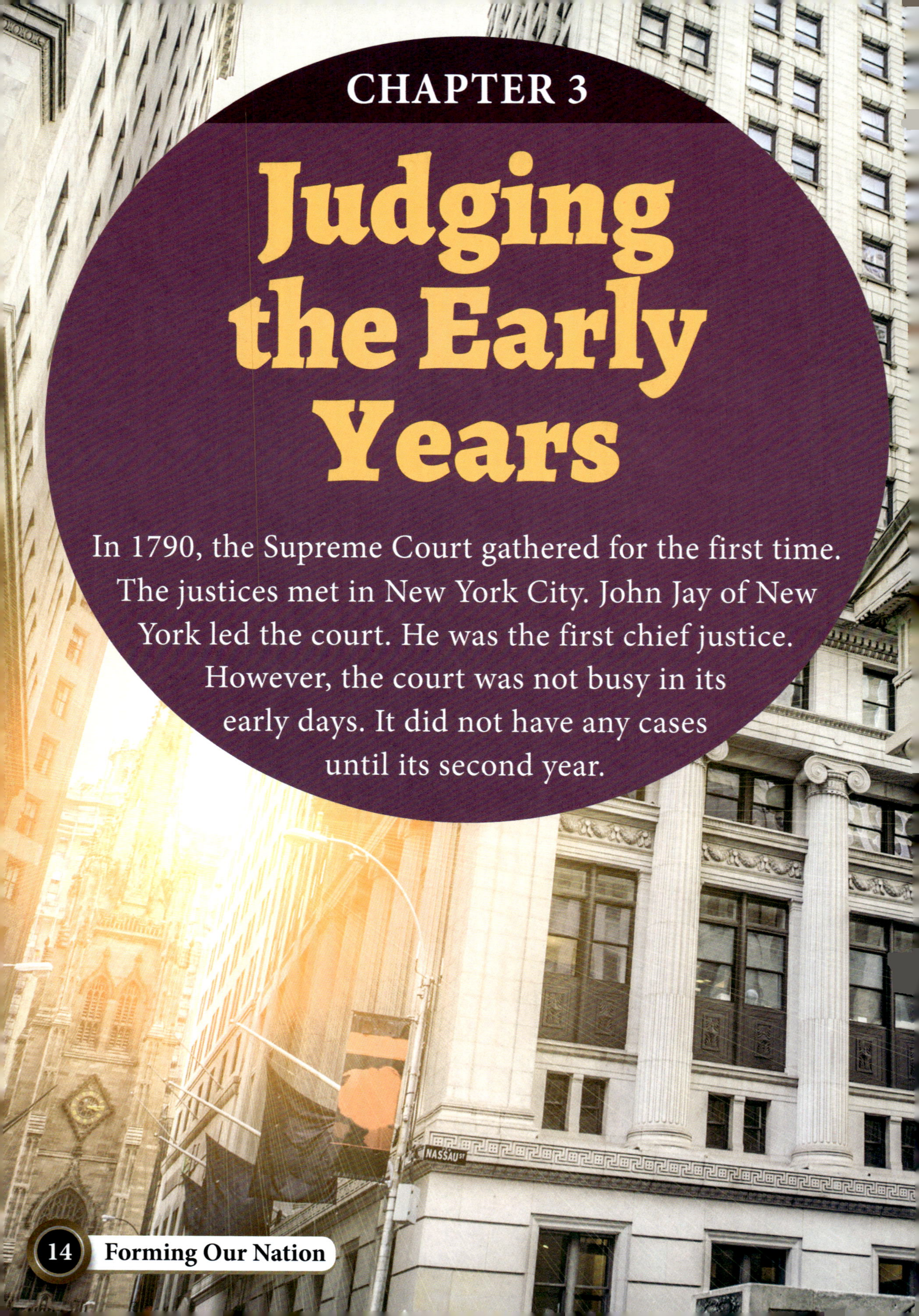

Federal Hall was built as New York's City Hall in 1700. It later became home to the Supreme Court, Congress, and executive branch.

John Jay of New York served as the first chief justice from 1789 to 1795.

A case can reach the Supreme Court in different ways. The most common is when someone **appeals** a lower court's decision. Another way is when the Supreme Court decides to review a state court's decision relating to the Constitution. The Supreme Court can also rule on disagreements between states.

The Supreme Court justices had few cases in the early 1790s. But they were still busy. They had to attend the circuit courts. To do so, they had to travel many miles in the winter months. They often had to go over rough roads. Many early justices complained.

The first major Supreme Court decision came in 1793. The case was Chisholm v. Georgia. Years earlier, the state of Georgia had ordered supplies from a man in South Carolina. Georgia received the supplies but never paid. The South Carolina man's relatives wanted to sue Georgia in the Supreme Court.

James Iredell was one of the first Supreme Court justices. At 39 years old, he was the court's youngest member.

Georgia's lawyer did not think federal courts had **authority** over states. Georgia's leaders believed each state was **sovereign**. Many leaders in other states agreed with this idea. But the Supreme Court ruled against Georgia. The justices based their decision on the Constitution. It said states were under the power of the federal government. That meant the Supreme Court had authority over the states.

The ruling made state leaders upset. They did not like limits to their power. Members of Congress disliked the ruling, too. Less than two years later, Congress began the process of changing the Constitution. They wrote the Eleventh Amendment. It says states cannot be sued by people from other states. In 1795, the amendment became official.

CHAPTER 4

Power of Review

In 1803, the Supreme Court ruled on a case called Marbury v. Madison. The case involved lower-court judges. John Adams had recently lost the presidential election to Thomas Jefferson. But before leaving office, Adams had appointed many lower-court judges.

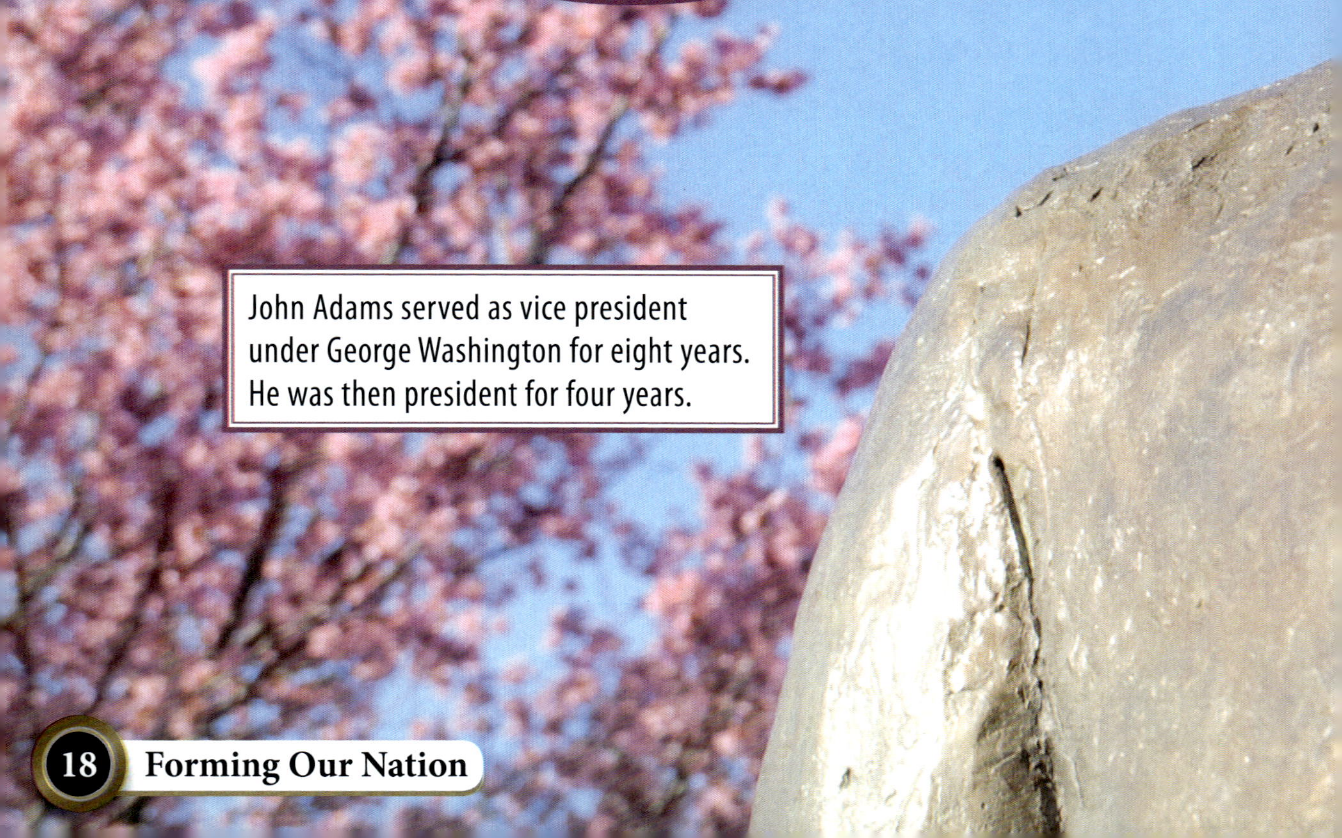

John Adams served as vice president under George Washington for eight years. He was then president for four years.

Thomas Jefferson served as the first secretary of state (1789–1794), second vice president (1797–1801), and third president (1801–1809) of the United States.

Jefferson disliked these judges. He decided to stop them from taking office. Jefferson told his secretary of state, James Madison, not to give the judges their papers. These papers would make their jobs official.

William Marbury was one of the judges. Marbury asked the Supreme Court for a legal order. This order would force Madison to give up the official papers. Several years earlier, Congress had passed a law granting the court this power. However, the Constitution did not grant the court this power.

The court ruled against Marbury. This decision **established** an important idea. If a law does not follow the Constitution, the Constitution overrules the law. This case was the first time a law passed by Congress was declared **unconstitutional**.

Jefferson had won. But he was not happy about the court's increased power. The court had shown that it could overrule laws made by Congress.

Supreme Court FACTS

The number of justices on the court has changed **six times**, from as few as 5 to as many as 10.

Of the **113 people** who have served on the Supreme Court, 2 have been **African American** and 4 have been **women**.

The first Supreme Court meeting was *delayed* by **one day**. Several justices could not make it on time.

John Marshall

John Marshall led the Supreme Court for more than 30 years. He wrote the court's decision for Marbury v. Madison. The case was important because it decided "whether an act [against] the Constitution, can become the law of the land."

Marshall believed the answer was clear. The ideas in the Constitution "are designed to be permanent," he wrote. In addition, "The powers of the legislature are . . . limited." Marshall said it was the "duty of the judicial [branch] to say what the law is." He explained that the courts must follow the Constitution, not ordinary laws. The other justices agreed. They voted **unanimously** against Marbury. It was the first time the Supreme Court struck down a federal law.

John Marshall was the chief justice from 1801 to 1835. He is considered one of the most influential Supreme Court justices of all time.

CHAPTER 5

The Modern Judicial Branch

As the United States increased in size during the 1800s, the Supreme Court increased in numbers. By 1863, there were 10 justices. Congress set the modern number, nine, in 1869. The number of district courts and circuit courts also increased.

The Supreme Court did not have its own building until the 1930s. Today, it is located in Washington, D.C., one block from the U.S. Capitol.

By the late 1800s, the Supreme Court was hearing about 400 cases a year.

The Supreme Court justices became busier, even though Congress established more circuit judges in 1869. More cases came up. Congress added one court of appeal for each circuit court. Laws limited the number of appeals that made it to the Supreme Court.

TIMELINE

IMPORTANT SUPREME COURT CASES

1819

In McCulloch v. Maryland with a 7–0 decision, the Supreme Court decides the Constitution gives the federal government powers over the states.

1857

With a 7–2 decision in Scott v. Sandford, the Supreme Court declares African American slaves are not U.S. citizens and cannot sue the federal government.

1896

During Plessy v. Ferguson, the Supreme Court decides 7–1 that states have a right to segregation laws, which keep people separate by race.

1954

The Supreme Court meets for Brown v. Board of Education and concludes with a 9–0 decision that state laws cannot separate schoolchildren by race.

Over time, the court has weighed in on many national issues. In some cases, the court has protected the rights of individuals. But the Supreme Court has not always acted to protect people's rights. In an 1896 ruling, the court supported laws that separated people by skin color. But in 1954, the court overturned this decision.

The Supreme Court will continue to affect the lives of people in the United States. As the third branch of the U.S. government, the court maintains the rule of law in the United States.

1963

The Supreme Court's 9–0 decision during Gideon v. Wainwright declares all people have the right to an attorney, even if they cannot afford one.

1966

In Miranda v. Arizona, the Supreme Court decides 5–4 that when making arrests, police must inform people of their rights, including their right to an attorney.

1974

With an 8–0 decision during the United States v. Nixon, the Supreme Court states that the president cannot withhold evidence from the courts.

2008

The Supreme Court maintains that people have a right to possess a firearm, including for self-defense at home, with a 5–4 decision during District of Columbia v. Heller.

2017

During Endrew F. v. Douglas County Schools, the Supreme Court decides 8–0 that a higher standard must be set for special education services offered by public schools to students with disabilities.

New London
1
Chester
2
King William
3
4
Edenton
Atlantic Ocean
Charleston
5
N
SCALE
0
190 Miles

Courts of the First States

In a few short years, the U.S. government created its own judicial system across the first 13 states. Many of the oldest courthouse buildings can still be visited today.

1

New London County Courthouse

New London, Connecticut

New London's courthouse was burned by the British during the American Revolutionary War. The new building, built in 1784, is the oldest courthouse in the state. It is currently home to the State of Connecticut Superior Court.

2

Chester County Courthouse

Chester, Pennsylvania

The Chester County Courthouse was built in 1724. It was the location of the first public reading of the Declaration of Independence. While no longer used as a courthouse, it is still home to important city and county events.

3

King William County Courthouse

King William, Virginia

The 1725 courthouse of King William, Virginia, is the country's oldest courthouse in constant use. The courthouse is located in a small town outside the state capital, Richmond. The rural setting was common for courthouses in the area, which were spread out among the large plantations of the South.

4

Chowan County Courthouse

Edenton, North Carolina

Edenton was the first permanent settlement in North Carolina. Its original courthouse was an important meeting place during colonial times. Its current courthouse was built in 1767 and has remained an important public building since then.

5

Charleston County Courthouse

Charleston, South Carolina

President Washington visited Charleston's courthouse in the early 1790s while looking for ideas for designing the White House. While there, he met architect James Hoban, who was hired for the job.

Quiz

1 Which body served as the U.S. government in 1783?

2 Who created the Virginia Plan?

3 Which branch of the government settles disagreements about the laws?

4 Did the Constitution explain how the federal courts would be set up?

5 Why were there 13 district courts?

6 Who chose the people to fill the first positions in the federal court?

7 How many cases did the Supreme Court have in its first year?

8 Who did not like the judges appointed by John Adams?

9 How many Supreme Court justices are there now?

10 Do laws limit the number of appeals that make it to the Supreme Court?

ANSWERS

1. The Congress of the Confederation **2.** James Madison **3.** The judicial branch **4.** No
5. There was one for each of the 13 states. **6.** President George Washington
7. None **8.** Thomas Jefferson **9.** Nine **10.** Yes

Key Words

appeals: asks a higher court to review a case

appointed: chosen for a job

authority: official power

established: created or set up

federal: having to do with the top level of government

independent: having the ability to make decisions without being controlled by another government

justices: people who hear cases in a court of law

sovereign: having the highest power

unanimously: having agreement from all members

unconstitutional: not following the Constitution

Index

LIGHTBOX

SUPPLEMENTARY RESOURCES

Click on the plus icon ⊕ found in the bottom left corner of each spread to open additional teacher resources.

- Download and print the book's quizzes and activities
- Access curriculum correlations
- Explore additional web applications that enhance the Lightbox experience

LIGHTBOX DIGITAL TITLES

Packed full of integrated media

VIDEOS

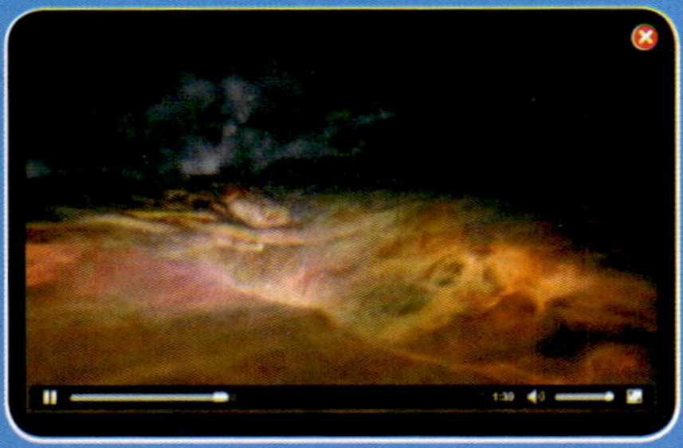

INTERACTIVE MAPS

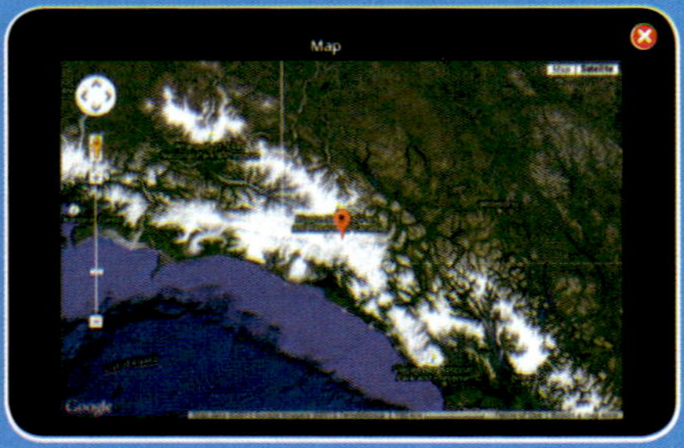

WEBLINKS

SLIDESHOWS

QUIZZES

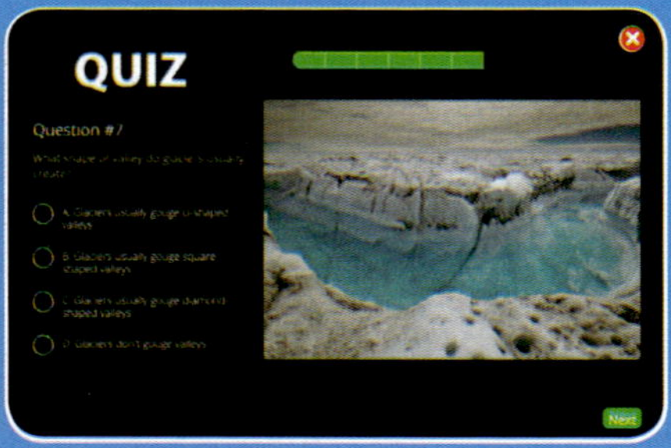

OPTIMIZED FOR

- ✔ TABLETS
- ✔ WHITEBOARDS
- ✔ COMPUTERS
- ✔ AND MUCH MORE!

Published by Smartbook Media Inc. 350 5th Avenue, 59th Floor New York, NY 10118
Website: www.openlightbox.com

First published by North Star Editions in 2018

Library of Congress Control Number: 2018936558

ISBN 978-1-5105-3797-2 (hardcover)
ISBN 978-1-5105-3798-9 (multi-user eBook)

Printed in Brainerd, Minnesota, United States
1 2 3 4 5 6 7 8 9 0 22 21 20 19 18

052018
111017

Project Coordinator Heather Kissock
Art Director Terry Paulhus

Photo Credits
Every reasonable effort has been made to trace ownership and to obtain permission to reprint copyright material. The publisher would be pleased to have any errors or omissions brought to its attention so that they may be corrected in subsequent printings.

The publisher acknowledges Alamy as its primary image supplier for this title.